Scottish Tartan Weddings: A Practical Guidebook

Scottish Tartan Weddings: A Practical Guidebook

ERIC MERRILL BUDD

HIPPOCRENE BOOKS, INC.
NEW YORK

All clan crest badge illustrations in Appendix A by Romilly Squire, heraldic artist in the Court of the Lord Lyon, King at Arms.

For information, address:
HIPPOCRENE BOOKS, INC.
171 Madison Avenue
New York, NY 10016

Cataloging in Publication Data available from the Library of Congress.

ISBN 0-7818-0754-9

Printed in the United States of America.

Acknowledgments

I would like to thank Chuck Swann, former editor of *The Gunn Salute* for printing my initial appeal for wedding stories and information; Larry Johnson, Southern California Branch Commissioner for the Clan Gunn Society of North America, who provided a plethora of facts and leads off the World Wide Web; Evelyn Murray, FSA (Scot.), of The Atholl Brose Scottish Imports; piper Leslie Paterson Webster; Jean Evans, Melody Lowman, Marté Matthews and Paul Means, and Shannon and Greg Maness who sent letters, articles and pictures; and a number of others who telephoned and discussed their weddings or the weddings of their friends and family. Also much appreciation to editor Kara Migliorelli and publisher George Blagowidow of Hippocrene Books, not only for putting this work into print, but for their commitment to printing quality books on the rich variety of ethnic traditions.

Contents

Introduction

Between the joy of the marriage proposal (and acceptance) and the celebration of the wedding, there is a maze of details, planning and bills. If you go into a bookstore, you will find any number of wedding advice books to help you through the whole process. But, if you are also planning a *tartan* wedding—complete with kilts, bagpipes and Scottish traditions—you would find very little help.

Until now.

This book is written to help with organizing a tartan wedding, a wedding filled with romantic charm and resplendent pride. I have researched the ins and outs of putting a wedding together, the etiquette of wearing the kilt and tartan, and the customs and lore of Scotland. This research not only included books, periodicals and the Internet, but also letters and phone calls from various people who have done their own tartan weddings. None of this necessarily makes me an expert on the subject. My role is as an editor, sifting and putting information together from various sources into a more convenient format. This is not intended as a definitive blueprint, but as a resource from which you the reader can pick and choose. My suggestion is to read the entire book at the beginning of your planning process, then discuss how you would like to conduct your wedding.

My interest in Scottish tartan weddings started when I began to wear the kilt on a more regular basis, usually when attending church. Wearing a kilt in the middle of Boston—especially when you don't play bagpipes—often provokes questions and conversation about things Scottish. One of the most frequent topics was that of tartan weddings, and I found myself relatively unprepared to respond. So, I began to look for information here and there, often struggling to find anything, and as I did the thought kept recurring: "There ought to be a book about this!" And this is the result.

Scots are also known for practicality, and this book is no exception. It is not enough to say "throw on a kilt, bring in the piper, and toss some coins to the kiddies." Brides and grooms need *workable* advice for planning the biggest event of their lives. My goal therefore has been to weave descriptions of tradition and Highland attire with useful information for putting together any kind of wedding.

Finally, in reflecting upon the Scottish tartan wedding, Shannon Maness offers the best advice that anyone could: "Our ancestors had many wonderful traditions that can be used, but a couple should not forget that the tartan wedding is not only a reflection of the past but of the couple and their style as well." This sentiment was echoed in many of the stories I heard, where old ways were woven together with creative expression and practical problem-solving.

As they say in the old country, *fair fa' ye twa, an' that's nae fleaching*—sincere good wishes to you both.

The Basics

You are getting married, and you cannot help but be excited. Now, take a deep breath and face reality. Planning a wedding is a huge affair—essentially putting together a worship service, a banquet, a dance party, and a family reunion all in one day. Then there's the honeymoon!

So, how do you have a "perfect wedding" and still keep your sanity? Everything I have read and heard, along with my personal experience helping to organize various events, suggests five basic principles to go by:

1. *Start early* – Most formal and semiformal weddings take at least a year to plan; smaller semiformal and informal ones may take less. The majority of that planning will take place in the first half of that year. Keep well-organized notes in a notebook or folder, or use one of the wedding planners sold in bookstores.
2. *Set a budget and stick with it* – Your bottom line should be within reason, taking into account what the two of you and your respective families are willing and able to contribute. The number of guests and the level of formality are the two factors that will determine cost the most. So will the season in which you choose to marry; summer and Christmas are the most expensive, especially on a Sunday, while fall and early spring are the least. Call

around and get price estimates, which can vary from one area of the country to the next. And don't forget to budget for your honeymoon, too.

3. *Discuss, don't debate* – Expect to make some compromises, both in style and in cost. You and your intended spouse should discuss and decide ahead of time what is important to both of you. As for advice from other people, that is just what it is: advice, not an obligation. This is *your* wedding, and no one else's. Whether you are negotiating with professionals or your future in-laws, be diplomatic but firm.
4. *Get it in writing* – When dealing with *any* professional, make sure that you have all of the essential terms spelled out in a contract, letter of agreement or print order. Ask for references, audition tapes, or portfolios whenever appropriate.
5. *Take care of yourself* – Stressful times are when you most need to eat right and get plenty of rest and recreation. Set aside some regular "R and R" time, just the two of you, so that you can recharge your batteries, enjoy yourselves, and remind each other why you are going through all of this in the first place.

A word about bridal consultants (also "wedding coordinators," or some combination of these terms). These are professionals who coordinate and mediate the details between the couple and the various vendors and service providers. There is even a national professional group, the Association of Bridal Consultants (see under "References and Resources"). It can be a great idea to hire one, but you may have to educate that person about Scottish customs, music and attire. If a particular consultant does not respect your heritage or your choices, find another one. If there are none in your area who will plan accordingly, then you may have to go it alone.

Finally, there is the all-important question of what makes a *tartan* wedding. The most prominent features are the wearing of tartan—especially the kilt—and bagpipes as part of the music. These are the most distinctive and colorful hallmarks of Scotland's cultural heritage. Many couples include handfasting as part of the ceremony, and some brides add heather and tartan ribbon to their bouquets. There are also Scottish customs and symbols that overlap with other cultures; Scots interacted considerably with the English, Irish, French and Scandinavians. In turn, Scottish settlers had a significant impact in the shaping of our North American culture. How much or little "Scottish-ness" you want in your wedding is, of course, up to you.

Courtship and Engagement

"O, I had wooers aught or nine,
They gied me rings and ribbons fine
And I was fear'd my heart wad tine,
And I gied it to the weaver."
—"The Gallant Weaver" by Robert Burns

First comes love, then comes marriage . . . whether in Scotland or any other land. Love grows with dating and courtship, getting to know one another, and leads to betrothal or engagement. Here, I will describe some of the courting and betrothal traditions of old Scotland, and how some might be adapted to modern times.

Meeting and Courting

The Scottish countryside was sparsely populated with few passable roadways, limiting the opportunities for finding a marriage partner. One of those opportunities was the country fair, where farmers and merchants traded, and young men found work for the season. The fairs were often a celebration, with games and horse racing, and thus became suitable venues for flirting and pairing up. Holy feast days, when church services were held in the open air, were other chances to meet one another. In larger towns, there were dances and holiday gatherings where lads and lasses got together.

Love Tokens

Often a young man would give "fairings"—small presents or tokens of affection—to his beloved. They included sweets, colored ribbons for her hair, or small items of jewelry. Couples would often carve their initials into a tree or stone, a custom dating from the ancient Druidic belief that certain stones and trees had magical properties, including the power over wishes and promises made upon them.

Of course, carving initials nowadays can get you into trouble, but fairings are always welcome. Hair ribbons could be blue (the color of Scottish heather, and symbolic of fidelity), tartan, or your beloved's favorite color. Chocolates and other candies can be easily obtained, but if you have a talent for baking, try your hand at making sweetmeats like Eyemouth tarts or Fochabers gingerbread.

Betrothal or Engagement

When a couple decided to get married, there was a formal asking. The groom-to-be would approach the father of his intended bride and ask for her hand, discussing his "prospects" for supporting her and their children. This would not be countenanced today, as it was certainly one-sided, but it did make some sense in a subsistence culture.

In the past, engagement was considered a binding contract. Couples were required to pay a pledge to the church, called "cryin' siller." This would be forfeited to the poor box if the wedding was called off, or in the event of a penny wedding or other "profane" behavior.

One form of asking was a *rèiteach.* It is still practiced in the Gaelic-speaking Outer Hebrides. It is a game-like ritual where a friend of the intended groom—who would often serve as best man—negotiated getting permission from the father of the bride, in a very subtle yet complex way.

Here is how it goes. Ian and Màiri are thinking of getting married. There is a gathering at Màiri's family's house, and after some talking Ian's best friend Alasdair raises a question to Màiri's father Angus: "I hear, sir, that you have a wee ewe lamb that needs caring for?"

"Aye," Angus replies, "that she does, though I care for her well enough as it is."

"Well, sir," Alasdair proposes, "I know someone who'd care for the wee lamb very well indeed. He has fine prospects, you see, and a good head on his shoulders."

Angus sips a bit of his whisky and thinks a while. "A kind heart, as well? I'll not be trusting this lamb to any cold-hearted beastie."

Alasdair shakes his head and assures him, "Don't you fear, sir. No kinder lad would you know in all your days."

"A kind lad, then, and hard-working to provide for his kin?"

"Aye, sir, that he is, sir."

Now Angus leans back in his chair, drumming his fingers on his glass. "Well, I may see this lad caring for my lamb yet—but only if she's fond of him."

There is a big grin on Alasdair's face. "Oh, I know there'll be no trouble there, sir!"

Chuckles and giggles follow his answer. Finally Angus accepts the proposal with a nod, and then the fiddler appears and the gathering turns into a celebration.

Nowadays, of course, you don't need anyone's permission to marry. But, imagine staging a rèiteach for a gathering of friends and family, perhaps even with costumes and Scots accents. They would watch and listen, somewhat amused and very bewildered, until the "kindhearted lad" and the "wee lamb" stand together; he proposes, she accepts, he slips the ring on her finger, and now everyone is delighted to be in on the joke. And you have not only announced the engagement, but you have set the tone for the wedding *and* had some fun doing it.

Another alternative is to do a *handfasting* ceremony. In old Scotland, handfasting was a legally and socially recognized form

Shannon and Greg Maness being handfasted by the Reverend Bill Gupton.

of trial marriage. The couple would stand before witnesses, join hands and recite some simple vows. They would then be married for a year and a day, after which they had the choice of parting company or marrying for keeps.

A more contemporary option is sending out "save the date" cards to friends and extended family. This is not the same as a formal invitation, but simply says:

Please save the date of
Friday, the sixth of April
for the wedding of
Màiri Ealasaid MacInnes
and
Ian Raibeart Ferguson
in Aberdeen, Washington.
Scottish Highland attire suggested.
Invitation to follow.

This is definitely a convenient option for friends and family who are scattered all over the map. Also, the added note about attire allows people time to prepare.

Tocher and Trousseau

A bride's family often provided a *tocher*, or dowry, when she married. It could be a sum of cash, cattle or sheep, or some other items of value. This was a way of contributing to her future household, and of binding the families together. The bride-to-be would also have a *trousseau*—more commonly called a "bottom drawer" of linens, blankets and other furnishings. These were often gathered by her female kin, or even neighbors in the village or town.

Weddings in the country were often a communal affair, with everyone pitching in. Many people made and gave "wee mindings"—wooden or wicker utensils for the bride's new household. Women would gather for a "hen night" where chickens were plucked and prepared for the wedding feast—now modified into a girl's night out on the town, like today's bachelorette party.

Luckenbooth and Wedding Ring

The diamond engagement ring has become a standard in American culture. In fact, the nearly exclusive use of the diamond for this purpose is a recent invention, created by the marketers of DeBeers, Tiffany's and other diamond sellers. Prior to that, engagement rings came with all sorts of precious and semi-precious stones: emeralds, pearls, garnets, amethysts, and so forth. You may be familiar with the Irish claddagh rings, showing a heart with a crown on top framed by two hands. The claddagh is used in other jewelry and decorations as well, and there are even rings with diamonds set in the heart for engagement rings. While it has been adopted by many people regardless of their cultural background, it is still seen as a distinctively Irish motif.

Scots have a similar betrothal symbol as well: the Luckenbooth. This is usually a brooch in the form of two interwoven hearts with a coronet crown on top, sometimes flanked by two doves. The name comes from the jeweler's locked stall or booth in Edinburgh's market where they were frequently sold. The Luckenbooth has also been incorporated in other jewelry, including rings. The "Young Pretender" Charles Edward Stuart, also known as Bonnie Prince Charlie, had given such a ring to his mistress Clementina Walkenshaw; it is now in the Inverness Museum and Art Gallery in Scotland. Stylized variations of the Luckenbooth can be found in brooches, pendants, rings, and other jewelry.

Another motif often used for engagement rings and wedding bands is a Celtic knot design. This consists of two or more strands woven together in a repetitive pattern to form an intricate circle. A simpler form is the trefoil knot, consisting of a single strand woven into a knot with three outer leaf-shaped loops. The Celtic knot was frequently used in ancient metalwork and stone relief carvings, symbolizing continuity and eternity. Many jewelers offer silver and gold Celtic knot design bands as wedding rings, and they have become very popular both in America and in the British Isles.

An added touch is to have the inside of the ring engraved. You may choose a line from Robert Burns or Byron, or perhaps a phrase with personal meaning for the both of you. Another option is a saying in Scots Gaelic. Here are a few phrases to consider:

Is gradhaich leam thu – "I love you."
Is thu m'annsachd – "Thou art my most beloved."
Mo ghaol ort – "My love with you."
Mo ghràdh bithbhuan – "My love forever."
Mo rùn geal dìleas – "My faithful fair one." (also the title of a Gaelic love song)
Tha gaol agam ort – "[My] love is with you."

Some examples of wedding bands with Celtic knot designs. The Celtic knot symbolizes the complex continuity of life.

Choosing a Location

While most Scottish weddings were performed in a church, they could and did take place just about anywhere. The venue reputedly most often used for weddings was the blacksmith's shop in the town of Gretna Green, Scotland's southernmost mainland locale. Because Scots law made marriage easier and at a younger age, many English couples would elope to Gretna Green, crossing the border and marrying "owre the iron"—with hands joined over the blacksmith's anvil for luck. Prior to the Protestant Reformation, many weddings were held on the church steps, followed by a nuptial mass in the sanctuary, and the wedding feast lasting well into the night. Weddings were also conducted in homes and castles, fishing boats and fairgrounds, wherever two people could join hands and recite their vows before witnesses.

You may already know where you want to get married, or you may not have a single clue. Either way, or any way in between, there are some important questions you should ask for both the ceremony and reception sites:

1. *Size* – What is the seating capacity of the sanctuary or main room? What about other rooms, which may be used for preparing, dressing, or childcare?
2. *Condition* – Is the building sound? How does it look, inside and out? Will there be renovations or repairs before the wedding? What about acoustics for music? This is especially

a concern for bagpipes, which sound better in a large, open space.

3. *Cost and restrictions* – What are the fees involved? Is there a contract or letter of agreement, and does it spell out all of the rules and restrictions for using the site? If you are considering a house of worship, talk to the prospective officiant. What about religious requirements for the ceremony? How flexible (or rigid) are they about written vows, attire, music, and so forth?
4. *Access* – Are there ramps, chair lifts or other amenities to make the site more accessible for disabled and elderly guests?
5. *Lighting and sound* – Can the site provide the lighting you desire? Does the sound system work well? If there isn't any, and you need to hook one up, can the power system handle the equipment? Are there staff connected with the site who can operate lights and sound equipment?
6. *Reception hall and kitchen* – If this is a church, is there another large room with a kitchen that can be used for the reception? If the church does not have such a place available, is there another place nearby? Can a reception hall be used for both the ceremony and reception?
7. *Dressing rooms* – Are there places at the site, or nearby, where the wedding party can get dressed?
8. *Piper's room* – Bagpipers need to tune up their instruments before performing, so look for a suitable place at or near the site for your piper to do this.

Of course, you may decide to choose an outdoor wedding, which is very much in keeping with Scottish customs. Marriage vows often were made over sacred stones, a remnant from ancient Druidic beliefs, and handfastings were done at country fairs and other open-air gatherings. Even weddings at the bride's home were more often done out-of-doors, with the reception taken inside. Outdoor weddings also have their negatives, the most obvious being the weather. I advise coming up with a backup plan, such as having the reception indoors and nearby, and reserving the reception hall for the full time.

Speaking of the reception, you will want to ask some important questions. Is it close to the ceremony, and easily accessible? How large is it? Is dancing allowable? What about catering, liquor, furnishings, and cleanup? When talking to the manager of a reception site, the more you are told "we can't do that," the more inclined you should be to look for another place.

Bring Furrit the Tartan!

A Brief History of Tartan

When most people think of tartan, they think of the myriad plaid patterns worn on scarves, skirts and flannel shirts. But, tartan is also an important symbol of Scottish culture and identity, and of the survival and resilience of the Highlanders.

Records of Celtic peoples using something akin to tartan go back to the days of the Roman Empire. An excavation near Falkirk revealed among the relics a well-preserved piece of woven wool cloth, showing a checkered twill pattern like that of the Rob Roy tartan. From a distance, such a cloth could remind one of Vergil's remark in the *Aeneid* of the Celt's "shining striped cloaks." The Gaels and other Celts were observed to wear close-fitting wool leggings, like the *trews* or tartan breeches now worn by some. At some point—probably during the Viking incursions—the Scottish Gaels adopted a single-piece wrap-around garment.

Weavers used local plants to dye the wool, and wove them into more and more complex line patterns. While certain colors and patterns may have been popular in particular regions, there is no solid evidence that a system of clan tartans had developed and persisted throughout the ages. To the contrary, portraits show many Highlanders wearing clothes made of two or more tartans.

There is also a story that demonstrates how Highlanders were identified. After the battle of Culloden, British troops came across a wounded Highlander and were about to finish him off when the man cried out that he was a Campbell (one of the clans loyal to King George). The soldiers replied that they didn't know this *because he wasn't wearing his bonnet*. But, there was no mention of his tartan, which he surely must have been wearing since they could tell he was a Highlander. The bonnet, on the other hand, was adorned with a plant badge identifying his clan tucked into a cockade of colored ribbon (black or red for the loyal troops, white for the Jacobite rebels).

So, how did the present schema of clan tartans come about? Let us go back in history, to 1688. The Dutch William of Orange and his British wife Mary accepted the throne after the removal of Mary's father, James VII and II. However, many Catholics and some Episcopalians in Scotland still supported the House of Stuart, and thus a resistance movement was formed called the Jacobites. James' son would make two abortive attempts to regain the throne, with foreign aid and Highland volunteers, but the Jacobites were too small in number and too poorly prepared to make any difference. Then along came James' grandson, Charles Edward Stuart, also called "the Young Pretender" and "Bonnie Prince Charlie." He led another uprising in 1745 and, while he had little or no chance for success, the British took it as a very serious threat. At the battle of Culloden in 1746, the Duke of Cumberland routed Charlie's troops—most of them Highland Gaels dressed in tartan kilts. The Young Pretender escaped, but the British Parliament soon ordered that no common man or boy should be allowed to wear the kilt or anything made from tartan cloth. In effect, an entire people were punished for the armed resistance of a small minority.

The Proscription crippled trade in tartan, and likely a number of patterns were lost. But the law was unevenly enforced, and Highland army regiments were still permitted to wear kilts. Each regiment had its own particular tartan, most of them variations on the Black Watch pattern. With the Jacobite movement virtually extinguished, and the interest in Highland culture renewed, the Proscription was lifted in 1782. By the beginning of the nineteenth century, a romantic revival had further increased interest in the Highlands and tartan. The leader in the revival, Sir Walter Scott, supervised the state visit of King George IV in Edinburgh, with every Scottish noble both Lowland and Highland wearing kilt and tartan, and His Majesty himself swathed in red Royal Stuart. While the initial reaction was shock and revulsion—many still regarded Highland garb as relics of a "barbaric" culture—soon the symbolic and commercial value of tartan was recognized, and *everyone* had to have a tartan! Drawing on the concept of regimental tartan, many began to assume that there were corresponding tartan patterns designated for clans and families. This was also fed by the tendency of mills to apply names to various patterns, including the names of clans and families. There was also an attempt to document clan tartans by the Highland Society of London.

Then, along came a pair of brothers who made two astounding claims. The first claim was that they were the long-lost grandsons of Bonnie Prince Charlie and Princess Louisa Sobieska, hence they called themselves John and Charles Sobieski Stuart. The second was that they possessed an ancient manuscript documenting the original clan tartans in detail, which they published as the *Vestiarium Scotium*. Now the brothers could not prove their claims—in fact there was plenty of evidence to the contrary—but people wanted to believe them and did. It seems that this tradition was sustained more by belief than by cold hard fact. Nonetheless, people of Scottish ancestry still continue to wear clan tartans, as the tradition uniquely serves to bind a community together.

In the 1960s, the Scottish Tartans Society was founded to act "as a worldwide authority on tartans and Highland dress." The Society maintains a Registry of All Known Tartans, a library and archives, and two museums in Edinburgh and in Franklin, North

Carolina. You can even retain the Society to design a new tartan for a group or special occasion, including having it recorded in the Registry.

Choosing a Tartan

Choosing the tartan for your wedding can be critical for the color scheme of the decorations. Clans often have more than one version of their tartan: modern, ancient, hunting, and dress. Your clan's modern tartan may look dark and somber, or incredibly garish for your tastes, but the hunting or ancient colors may be perfect. There is also *arisaid*, a white-background tartan intended for ladies' wear, but also worn by men; many dress tartans are in fact arisaid. For some larger clans, such as Campbell and MacDonald, there may be several tartans depending on which branch you belong to. Also, there is the MacAlpin tartan but no true MacAlpin clan; however, the Grant, MacAulay, MacFie, MacGregor, MacKinnon, MacNab and MacQuarrie clans are said to share common descent from this ancient family, so the MacAlpin tartan is a possible alternative.

Things can get more complicated if each of you is Scottish from a different clan, and you now have two tartans (or groups of tartans) from which to choose. I am no master at interior decoration, so I will not pretend to guide you, but your two major colors will likely be the base color of each family's tartan. Again, if the modern colors of a tartan are not to your liking, or they do not go well with the other tartan, look at another color scheme.

Now, who wears which tartan? If John is of the Campbell clan and Pat doesn't even have any Scottish ancestors, then everyone wears Campbell. But, if Pat is MacLeod, she may choose to wear her tartan. To coordinate everything, John's best man and groomsmen would wear kilts in Campbell tartan, while Pat's maid of honor and bridesmaids would wear MacLeod tartan sashes. And what about all the guests? Well, none of them are obligated to wear tartan, but if they choose to, then those of Scottish background wear the tartan associated with their respective clan, family, or ancestral district. If not, guests can still choose from a number of general and district tartans. General (or "universal") tartans include Hunting Stewart, Black Watch, Caledonian, Jacobite, Scottish National Dress, Braveheart Warrior (dress and hunting colors), Flower of Scotland, Pride of Scotland, and Universal Ancient International. There are also three tartans associated with the United States: American, American Bicentennial (also called American Saint Andrews) and American Eagle. There are also district tartans for Alabama, Arkansas, California, the Carolinas, Georgia, Maine, Ohio, Oklahoma, Texas, Vermont and Washington state. For Canadians, there is a Maple Leaf tartan and separate tartans for each province. People of Irish ancestry can choose the Irish National tartan, or the tartan representing the county where their ancestors came from.

The bagpiper and the officiant are next. Bagpipers usually have kilts and plaids in one or more tartans, and there is a special Clergy tartan (in both blue and green) for religious officiants. For a secular officiant, such as a judge, the black robe will be fine—but if the judge is also Scottish and wants to wear his or her own tartan, all the better!

Decorating the Wedding Site

So, with your tartans straight, how do you dress up the ceremony and reception sites? Generally the more formal the wedding, the more ornate the decoration. However, you don't necessarily need to dress up an already wonderful looking church or reception hall. My best advice is to consult with a florist, floral or party designer, or event planner. Do a site search and discuss what you want and need. Some designers will do free consultations, others will charge a consult fee.

There are a couple of tips I can offer for adding a Scottish touch to your decorations.

With bouquets and floral arrangements, add blue heather (for Scotland), your clan or family plant badge (see Appendix A for a listing), or both. Professionals also advise that you choose your flowers according to the season, and stay clear of overly fragrant blossoms.

Bows and ribbons offer a simple but elegant touch. If your tartan is a commonly used one like Stewart or MacLeod, then you may very likely find matching tartan ribbon; otherwise, you will have a long hunt. Another alternative is to use ribbons in the different colors of the tartan, or simple blue and white for the Scottish national flag. Keep in mind, however, that the tartan you and the rest of the wedding party wears is the most Scottish display you will have, and the one all eyes will most be admiring. So, my personal advice is to keep it simple and tasteful.

Invitations and Other Printing

In the Highlands of old, printed wedding invitations were unnecessary. Weddings were a community event, and everyone participated in some way or another. In larger towns, the bridesmaids went about inviting guests by word of mouth. But, with modern times and mobility, and with weddings becoming more formal and lavish, sending invitations has become standard practice for bringing everyone together.

So, now that you know when and where, the next step is who to invite. Chances are you will have at least two lists—one for the ceremony, and one for the reception. Scots weddings often are divided into the ceremony, a dinner with close friends and family, and a dance in the evening with more guests. If you decide to separate your reception in this way, you might want to have some drinks and light snacks at the dance. Lastly, you may also wish to send announcement cards to people whom you know cannot attend.

First, decide how many people you will invite, then choose who will be on the lists. On the top of the list are immediate family, members of the wedding party and close mutual friends. Remember to talk to your parents about who should be included. You will likely have to trim down your initial list, and the sooner you begin the better. If you have a home computer, you can use database software or a word processor's "mail merge" function to sort and generate printed lists. And remember to keep these lists *after* your wedding, for sending thank-you notes and holiday greetings.

The next step is drafting the copy for invitations and announcements. Standard copy usually reads as follows:

Mr. And Mrs. Angus MacInnes
request the honour of your presence
at the marriage of their daughter
Màiri Ealasaid
To
Mr. Ian Raibeart Ferguson
Friday, the sixth of April
at three o'clock in the afternoon
Saint Andrew's Church
Aberdeen, Washington
and reception afterwards
in the parish hall

Formal announcements are often worded:

Mr. And Mrs. Angus MacInnes
are pleased to announce
the marriage of their daughter
Màiri Ealasaid
to
Ian Raibeart Ferguson
Friday, the sixth of April

There are, of course, numerous variations according to rules of etiquette:

1. While "request the honour of your presence" is correct when the wedding is in a church or other place of worship, "request the pleasure of your company" is advised for weddings at a secular venue.
2. For the time of day, print "half past three o'clock" instead of "three-thirty"; spell out numbers, and always include the words "o'clock" at the end of the time. It is also a good idea to distinguish morning, afternoon or evening.
3. The bride's name always goes before the groom. When her parents are hosting the wedding, there is no "Ms." or "Miss" before her name, but "Mr." appears before his; when the groom's parents are hosting, this rule is reversed. When both sets of parents are hosting, you can either drop the titles or put them in for both. Titles should be used for both when the couple host their own wedding.
4. For a reply, print "RSVP" or "The favour of a reply is requested." It is recommended that couples ordering invitations have response cards with return envelopes printed up, and the date by which the person should reply (about three to four weeks before the wedding). It is not only more convenient for the prospective guests, but easier on the couple receiving them.

There are a myriad of other details in wording—when the bride's parents are divorced and remarried and all four are hosting the wedding, and so forth. Most printers have an etiquette chart to help you follow these rules, and are more than happy to help. Informal weddings do not require such formal language on their invitations, including the British "honour" and "favour" instead of American spellings. Still, for a Scottish theme, I would keep these British forms, even for a small wedding in the family garden.

Printers will often do complete sets of invitations, announcements, envelopes, response cards and wedding programs. These are not only convenient, but less expensive overall. Shop around for price, quality and convenience before placing your order. Ask if you can see proof copies before the full set is printed; this may add to the cost, but it is a worthy investment if you are doing a complicated printing job. When you place your final order, make sure you have an extra twenty-five sets or so, just to be on the safe side, and get a copy of the print order. Expect a minimum of two weeks for the print order to come through.

For a special touch, you may want to add some graphics to your printing. Full-color tartan borders would be wonderful, but the cost will be very high. Another alternative is to have your clan crest badge printed or embossed at the top; this will likely be considered a custom item and therefore costly, but much less so than printing your tartan. Other possible motifs are the Scottish thistle, a bagpiper, or the Luckenbooth emblem. A printer may have any of these motifs available, or you might need to provide them for an extra cost. If you or someone you know has a home computer and some talent, you can do the layouts and provide floppy discs to the printer, which can cut down on both expense and time. Make sure that the computer format you use is compatible with what the printer uses.

You may also decide to print out the invitations, announcements and programs yourself. As someone who has worked in printing, copying and desktop publishing, I would recommend that you think carefully about it. Certainly printing at home can be cheaper, and perhaps even quicker, but you may not get the quality you desire. Some papers and card stocks which are appropriate for invitations will not run well through a laser or ink jet printer, or may warp or bend.

Another do-it-yourself touch is to add ribbons to the invitation. If you can find your tartan in ribbon, you can make bows and attach them to the cards. This can require a lot of labor and time, and can be messy if you decide to glue them on. My suggestion is to cut two small slits in the top center, thread a piece of ribbon through them and tie it into a bow.

Consider also sending out an information sheet. This is something you can type up and copy yourself. On one side would be details about Scottish attire and tartan accessories, including where people could buy or rent them. Give people a full and accurate range of options, from a simple tartan necktie or scarf, to a kilt with evening dress. On the other side, have a map or written directions to the ceremony and reception. Make sure these directions are clear and easy to follow, and include descriptions of obvious landmarks. You might include this information sheet with the invitations, or simply wait for the RSVPs and send it out then.

What to Wear: The Lasses

"She stood in her snood and arisaid
Beneath the trees of the wood,
The buckled plaid round her shoulders laid,
She looked for him as she stood."
—from a Scots Gaelic love poem

This chapter will cover six things: the bride's wedding gown, the bridal headdress, the tartan sash, the bridesmaids' attire, bouquets and corsages, and attire for guests. I will not pretend to be an expert on women's fashion, and instead leave it to you to choose what suits your tastes.

The Wedding Gown

The "traditional" white wedding gown is, in fact, a recent invention. It first caught on during the latter part of the nineteenth century, and became quite popular in the beginning of this century. Somewhere, at some point, a person asked why the bride was wearing white and not some other color. Instead of saying the truth—that it was a show of wealth at that time— somebody made up the answer that it was a sign of purity, and this reasoning has stuck ever since. Of course, traditions do have to start somewhere. My point is that you don't have to wear white if you don't want to. If you want to go further back in tradition, blue was a favorite color among Scottish brides, symbolizing fidelity: "married in blue, love ever true." The two colors that were *not* worn for pre-Victorian Scottish wedding dresses were green (because it could anger the faery folk) and black (because it symbolized death and mourning).

Whether you wear white or blue or otherwise, if your wedding is formal then you will be shopping for a dress. The best plan is to place your order at least six months in advance—not because it will take that long, but because there is always the chance that something can go wrong. Call different bridal shops and set up appointments. DO NOT come tripping in with a gaggle of friends and family! Aside from terrifying the poor merchants, you will create much more chaos for yourself. Keep your appointment and bring only one person whom you trust to help you with a decision. Do not be afraid to ask a lot of questions about fabric, style, workmanship, prices for the dress and alterations, and so on. And when trying on a dress—either for the first time or after the final fitting—move around in it so that you are sure it is comfortable.

There are, of course, alternatives to buying a new dress from a retail boutique. You could have your mother's or another relative's dress altered to fit you. A few places rent dresses, which is considerably cheaper; such places are hard to find, however, so you will have to do some research. There are mail-order and Internet retailers, but look carefully and seriously consider taking the dress to a restorer or seamstress in your area. Some brides-to-be have also found just what they were looking for hanging in the evening wear section of their local department store. Other options include consignment shops, some antique stores, and classified ads in your local newspaper.

Okay, you have found your wedding dress. Now come the accessories. They can include: headpiece, veil (of varying length), shoes, jewelry, gloves (optional), the customary blue garter, stockings and undergarments. The professionals in this business suggest that you purchase these items about a month before the wedding, but shop around well before that; they also recommend simple accoutrements with a more ornate dress, and vice versa.

The Headdress

While Scottish brides have increasingly worn hats and veils like other brides all over the world, this was not always the case. In medieval times, unmarried women would bind their hair in a *snood,* a strip of cloth that was tied about the head holding the hair in place. Upon being married, the bride then donned a *kertch*, a square of linen that was folded diagonally and draped over the head. In some places, the kertch was shaped like a three-pointed crown, the points symbolic of the Trinity. Gradually the snood and the kertch faded from use.

It was also common in the Highlands and islands for brides to wear garlands or wreaths either during or after the ceremony. Garlands were most likely made of seasonal wildflowers growing in the area, or from the boughs of certain trees or bushes. Willow and mistletoe were said to bring fertility, while rowan and elder warded away evil. Oak, the trees of the ancient Druids, was thought to be a very powerful talisman.

You might consider having a garland or wreath made for your headpiece. Consult with your florist about appropriate seasonal flowers and other materials, including the plant talisman of your clan. Wreaths can be more problematic than a simple garland, especially since they can start to feel heavy as time goes on. Think about trying a mockup of the wreath for fit and balance first.

The Tartan Sash

The woman's tartan sash is usually worn with evening wear, and it has developed a special role in many North American tartan weddings. Often when a groom of Scottish heritage marries, his family presents the bride with the sash as part of the ceremony. If the bride is also Scottish but of a different clan or family, she may trade her old sash for the new one given by her spouse.

Sashes are usually seven-and-a-half feet long, and eleven inches wide; wool ones can cost between thirty and fifty dollars, while silk sashes can run over one hundred dollars. Also, you will need a small brooch about one-and-a-half to two inches in diameter. You should *not* confuse a woman's sash and brooch with the much larger ones used by bagpipers.

There are several ways that a sash can be worn, according to a sophisticated code approved by Scotland's heraldic authority. For our purposes, I will describe the three that people are most likely to use. The most common style I will call the *standard crossover*. Start with one end of the sash at the front right waist, and swing it over your right shoulder and around your back to the left hip. Now bring the sash across the front and back over the right shoulder, and pin the sash to your dress where it crosses at the top of the shoulder. You should now have two ends loose, a short one in front and a long one in back; if this back end is too long, you can pin it to your waist or another part of the sash.

A second style is for women who marry out of their clan, but wish to wear their original tartan. The middle of the sash is pinned at the right shoulder, and the ends go across the front and back to the left hip, where they are tied in a large bow. This *bowed crossover* style is rarely seen, and may seem a bit garish for some.

The third style does not involve the sash crossing over the torso; instead it is folded to produce a *rosette* pattern which is then pinned to the right front shoulder. The folding is complicated, and along with the sash you will need a small brooch, a length of thread or string, two small safety pins and a larger safety pin. Here are the directions:

1. Fold the sash in half, either in equal lengths or with the longer end on the bottom. If there is a dull side to the sash, it should be on the inside.
2. Take the folded end and fold it over to make a square. Try to line up the tartan pattern so that one folded end mirrors the other.

Standard crossover method of wearing the ladies' tartan sash.

Tartan sash worn in bowed crossover style, the pattern for women who marry out of their clan but continue to wear their clan's tartan.

Paul Means and Marté Matthews at their cake cutting. The bride is wearing her Menzies tartan sash in a rosette.

3. Gather the square into pleats, and tie the string across the center. This may require two sets of hands, one to hold the pleats and one to tie the string. The end result should look like a double fan shape with the lengths of the sash emerging from one of the fans.
4. Bring the ends of the fans together and pin them from the bottom to create the rosette pattern. You may have to fold the edges underneath the rosette to make it lie flat. If you wish this to be permanent, you can sew the rosette together. The brooch is then pinned in the center front to hide the string. The large safety pin is attached to the string at the bottom to pin the rosette to the dress; the free ends of the sash go over the shoulder and down the back.

The main advantage of the rosette is that it can be made well ahead of time and then pinned to the bride before or during the wedding ceremony. Also, many Scottish country dancers prefer wearing the rosette—or some other style where the sash doesn't cross over the front—for ease and comfort.

A fourth and simpler approach is to fold the sash in half (as in step one of the rosette) and pin the folded end to the shoulder. This is not as decorative, but it is frequently seen. Personally, I prefer either the standard crossover or the rosette, but again I leave it to your tastes. Whichever way you choose to wear the sash, if you are going to have it put on you as part of the ceremony, I have three strong words of advice: *practice, practice, practice!* The standard and bowed crossover styles can become involved, especially in close quarters, and even pinning a rosette to the dress may need work to avoid bloodshed. Run through it several times until you have got it right, or at least so you can decide which way works best for you.

Finally, there is some controversy about wearing the sash on the right or left shoulder. Strictly speaking, according to Scotland's heraldic authority, ladies should wear the sash pinned to the right shoulder unless they are of high rank—for example, wives of clan chiefs and chieftains, and women who are chiefs or chieftains in their own right. The Royal Scottish Country Dance Society (RSCDS), however, has insisted on having the sash worn on the left shoulder, and not crossing the front of the dress. I have even heard rational explanations given for either side. The stricter, "wear-on-the right" school, points to the fact that men who wear shoulder plaids wear them on their *left* shoulder, and having the sash on the right strikes an aesthetic balance. On the other hand, some Scottish country dancers have claimed that, because the right arm is usually raised while dancing, it is therefore more comfortable to wear the sash on the left. Neither explains how this divergence of opinion began in the first place. My good friend Evelyn Murray—who is entitled to wear her sash on the left—has shared the following anecdote: One of the founders of the Scottish Country Dance Society, wanting to know how to wear the sash, asked a lady more familiar with the wearing of tartan. "Why, I wear it on the left shoulder," the lady answered—and so it has been that way ever since. The lady in question was the wife of a prominent chief, but she never elaborated on the right-left distinction, and since then many country dancers have favored the left shoulder. This may seem like a petty argument to most Americans, but even on this side of the Atlantic some people can and do argue about it. So, do not be surprised if you get conflicting advice about this, and even adamant insistence. My own view is to favor the right shoulder, but there is also a compromise that works well with the rosette: wear the sash on the right for the ceremony, and switch it to the left for dancing at the reception.

The Bridesmaids' Attire

Once again, I emphasize that I am not a fashion mogul. However, I am a good listener, and when it comes to bridesmaids' dresses I have heard many horror stories from female acquaintances.

Therefore, all I can say to you about selecting what your attendants will wear is to please avoid garish colors, incredibly puffy sleeves and skirts, excessive bows and frills, and anything else that would make your friends cringe. Talk to them first, and see if you can arrive at a consensus that everyone is comfortable with.

Here, then, are some modest proposals for deciding how to dress your maid of honor and bridesmaids:

1. According to people more in the know than myself, off-the-shoulder has become a popular fashion in bridesmaids' dresses. This is seemingly more attractive than the marshmallow-shaped sleeves of old, and no doubt must be more comfortable in warmer weather as well.
2. One option is to have simplified versions of your wedding gown made in another color.
3. There is also a formal tartan ensemble for women: white blouse with lace jabot and cuffs, black velvet or wool vest, tartan kilt-skirt, white stockings, and black Mary Jane shoes. This may look too "folksy" to some, but if it appeals to you and your friends it has the advantage of coordinating well with the attire of the male attendants.
4. If uniformity is not essential to you, consider this arrangement: pick a color and fabric that you and your attendants can agree upon, then give them each enough material to have a dress made in the style that they choose. You will likely have a different dress for each bridesmaid, but many brides who have done this were happy with the results. A word of caution: set some ground rules about what is not preferable, such as sequins and slits.
5. If you are thinking of having dresses made in tartan, I have two suggestions. First, tartan need not be worsted wool, but can be obtained in cotton or silk. Second, consider having the tartan cloth cut "on the cross"—that is, with the lines of the sett running diagonally instead of horizontal and vertical.

Example of a Scottish evening ensemble for ladies: tartan kilt-skirt, white blouse with lace jabot, black vest made in either wool or velvet, and black Mary Jane shoes. Illustration by the author.

Another item to think about is cost. You may pick the bridesmaids' outfits, but customarily they are the ones who pay for them. Keep their pocketbooks in mind, or be willing and able to pitch in.

Bouquets and Corsages

Flowers may not seem like attire, but they are an important part of your wedding ensemble. Most florists provide a *trousseau* or "package deal" arrangement where they do all of the flowers, from the groom's boutonniere to the garlands and altar arrangements in the church. To give him or her a better idea of what to work with, provide pictures of you and your bridesmaids, the wedding gown and the bridesmaids' attire. Also do the same for the mothers and grandmothers who will wear corsages at the wedding. Then the florist can create a bouquet that complements and fits in with the whole look. Again, talk about including Scottish flowers and greenery, notably blue heather and your clan or family plant badge. And do not be afraid to give him or her a "don't use" list—flowers that are too fragrant or garish, or which someone in the wedding party is allergic to.

Attire for Guests

The most well-known article of tartan apparel for women is the kilt-skirt, often worn with a white or pastel-colored blouse, and sometimes with a vest. I have also mentioned the tartan sash, which is especially encouraged for formal occasions. If the lady is a bit sheepish, or cannot afford such items, then a simple scarf or shawl in tartan will do. Encourage each guest to wear the tartan in whatever manner they choose, and make a special point to thank everyone who does.

What to Wear: The Lads

"Too great pains cannot be taken in putting on the kilt; no dress looks smarter when properly put on, and nothing worse when carelessly so."
– Dress Regulations of the Queen's Own Cameron Highlanders

The kilt is certainly one of the most distinctive ethnic attires in existence. Wear it on the street or in a restaurant, and people instantly recognize your heritage as Scottish. Combined with formal attire, there is no ensemble that makes any man look more dashing. So, if you are the groom and you are getting married in your kilt, consider yourself lucky indeed!

I am writing this chapter assuming that you are a neophyte to the ways of the kilt. If you are a Saxon (read, non-Scottish) groom marrying a Scottish lass, or you have been asked to serve as best man or groomsman at a tartan wedding, then this is the one part of the book you should not overlook. If you are of Scottish heritage and familiar with the ways of the kilt, this will simply be a refresher course.

The Scottish Highland kilt is centuries old. Originally, it was a large blanket folded and belted around the waist, and the upper part was pinned about the shoulders as a sash, or unfurled and used as cover for the rain or cold weather. At night, the kilt could be converted into something like a sleeping bag, so it was very convenient indeed. Sometime in the eighteenth century, the tailored modern kilt was created; the top portion was done away with, the pleats were sewn, and buckles and leather straps were added. This made it easier to put on and take off, and so this modern kilt (*feileadh beag*) replaced the older large kilt (*feileadh mor* or *breacan feile*).

The kilt is worn by wrapping it around your body and buckling it closed. Always put your shirt on before your kilt. The waistline comes around the bottom of the ribs, higher than your trouser waist. There is one buckle and a small belt hole on the left, and one or two buckles on the right. The pleated side is on the back, the right apron is folded over the front, the right leather strap is inserted in the belt hole and buckled to the left buckle, then the left apron folds over the right and is buckled. The kilt's hemline should be no lower than the top of your kneecap, and perhaps an inch above it.

When ordering the kilt, there are three things to keep in mind: fit, pleating and material. Most kilts are "made to measure," meaning that they fit the specific measurements of the owner. Some places will rent or sell kilts and kilt outfits by standard sizes, or "off the peg." If you are renting for one time, and you have a relatively average build, off the peg will do; if you are buying for long-term wear, and you are especially hard to fit, then invest in having it made to measure. As to pleating, most kilts are pleated "to the pattern" or "to the sett" to duplicate the sett of the tartan when the pleats lie flat. Some kilts are pleated "to the line" however, with the same segment of the tartan on each pleat; this is also called "military" pleating because it is more commonly used for Highland regimental uniform kilts. The material is typically worsted wool, of various weights from nine ounce to seventeen ounce. You will also see a mention of yardage—eight yards should be sufficient, but if you have a wider girth you may need nine yards. As for weight, it would depend upon how often you wear your kilt. If you will only wear it a few times a year, then nine to eleven ounce should suffice; if you are like me and wear the kilt at least once a week, then go for thirteen to seventeen ounce fabric. Two more points on quality. First, avoid saxony, which does not hold pleating well and will not last with wear. Second, make sure that you buy or rent your kilt from a reputable dealer, and not a costume shop.

What goes with the kilt? First, keep in mind that there are different levels of dress depending on the circumstances, just as you have "casual," "formal," and other modes for Saxon attire. "Day wear" ranges from totally casual to semiformal. You can wear T-shirts, sweaters and collared shirts with day wear, not to mention everything from sneakers to patent leather shoes. "Evening wear" is more formal, like a tuxedo with black tie. Jackets are made of black Barrathea wool, and shoes are either your typical black evening shoe or ghillie brogues. A step above evening wear is "full dress," equivalent to white tie and tails. Here, you wear a black doublet with either white tie or lace jabot, and shoes are either ghillies or silver-buckled Mary Janes. A fourth style is "Jacobean." This is a dress style reminiscent of 16th to 18th century attire, with an old-fashioned cross-laced shirt (much like so-called pirate shirts), a leather vest with shoulder tabs called a *peitean,* and similar accoutrements.

Here is a listing of all of the accessories that accompany a kilt, and the different variations according to mode of dress. For convenience, I will go from head to toe:

1. *Bonnet* – This is simply the Scottish headgear, of which there are two types: the Glengarry and the Balmoral. The Tam O'Shanter, or tam, is not really suitable with Highland attire, especially with formal wear. The Glengarry, which resembles the flat military day cap, is less popular than the beret-like Balmoral. For day wear, either one will do; for evening and full dress, stick with a black or dark navy blue Balmoral. On the left front of the bonnet is a patch of grosgrain ribbon called the *cockade*. You can leave this bare, but it looks more attractive if you wear a clan crest badge pin or other device. There are even generic "Scotland" badges, one with a thistle inside the circular strap-and-buckle, and another with the royal lion rampant.

The author in full dress attire—double-breasted Montrose doublet, lace jabot and cuffs, and shoulder plaid pinned with silver and amethyst brooch.

2. *Jackets* – Kilt jackets are cut with a higher bottom edge to accommodate the kilt's waistline, and have other touches with them. They almost always have military-style shoulder straps, for example. Day wear jackets are typically of the Argyll style, usually in tweed or wool of any color, and most often with plain cuffs and horn or plastic buttons. Evening wear is either a black Argyll or the more popular Prince Charlie, the latter having short tails in the back. Full dress means any of several doublets, the regulation doublet usually worn with white tie and white waistcoat, and the high-necked Sheriffmuir and Montrose worn with a lace jabot. Both evening wear jackets and full dress doublets have silver-plated buttons; the cuffs are usually either military (a rectangular panel with three widely-spaced buttons up the sleeve) or gauntlet (a large, thick cuff with three buttons across the top).
3. *Shoulder plaid* – The shoulder plaid is a remnant of the *breacan feile*. For day wear, a large folded plaid is thrown over the left shoulder. Fly or evening plaids, which are pinned to the left shoulder of the jacket and either tucked in the waist or left to hang loose, are worn with evening wear or full dress (more often the latter)
4. *Waistcoat and kilt belt* – Waistcoat is simply a vest adapted for kilt wear. The kilt belt is a wide leather belt, either brown or black, worn around the top of the kilt. As a general rule, you should never wear both a waistcoat and a belt together. If you are wearing a dirk, you will need a kilt belt, but you are unlikely to have a dirk unless you are in Jacobean attire or full dress. If you are wearing a belt with evening wear or full dress, it should be black with a silver-plate buckle. With the doublets (except the regulation), you will need to wear the belt.
5. *The delicate question* – Yes, it is true that most men who wear the kilt find it more comfortable without undergarments. Frequently a long-tailed shirt or oversized

Examples of kilt jacket sleeve cuffs: plain (left), military (center), and gauntlet (right).

undershirt is worn instead of briefs, and it is found more convenient when nature calls. Of course, some men may choose to have underwear, and in some cases (such as energetic dancing and athletic events) it would be more seemly to do so. In that case, many find bikini-style briefs to be easier to get in and out of. Whichever you decide, you will likely be asked by someone what is worn underneath, and we Scotsmen have one common answer: "Nothin' worn, all in first-class workin' order!"

6. *Sporran* – The sporran is a purse that hangs in front of the kilt from a small waist belt. For day wear, a plain or tooled leather sporran with a leather belt is best. For evening and full dress, the sporran should be fur with silver-plate fittings and a leather-and-chain belt. As part of Jacobean attire, simpler pouch sporrans have come back in vogue, but they are harder to find and often homemade. There is also an "animal-mask" sporran, a mask made of fur with the animal's head used as the cover flap, which can be worn with just about any mode of dress.
7. *Dirk* – The dirk is completely optional with full dress, and overly ostentatious with day or evening wear. Full dress dirks are often made with carved mahogany handles, silver fittings, and sheaths made of black leather over wood. They can be *very* expensive about as much or more as a complete kilt outfit. If you would like to use a dirk to slice your wedding cake, you do not need to wear one; your best man or another attendant can hand it to you or your bride when the time is right.
8. *Kilt pins* – These are for sheer decoration and not essential, but very nice to have with evening wear or full dress. The pin is worn on the lower right corner of the top apron. DO NOT pin it through both aprons, as this will cause the kilt to hang poorly. Pins range from simple ones resembling oversized safety pins, to miniature

swords with clan crest badges, to jeweled versions and the more ornate grouse foot pins bedecked with feathers and semiprecious stones. The only time kilt pins are not appropriate is with Jacobean wear, as the two are incongruous by at least one hundred years.

9. *Hose, garters and flashes* – Hose are usually woolen cuffed knee-high stockings, either white, shaded, diced or tartan. With more people of Scottish heritage living in warmer climates, many have turned to cotton and cotton/poly stockings for day wear; I myself have used soccer leggings for these occasions. Kilt hose are held up with garters, usually elastic bands with hook-and-eye fasteners worn under the cuff of the hose top. Garters also customarily come with flashes, which are decorative fabric tabs that peek out from under the cuff. There are also more elaborate castellated hose and tied garters, but these are harder to come by and rarely worn.
10. *Sgian dubh* – The *sgian dubh* is a short utility knife tucked in the right hose top (left if you are a southpaw). There are *sgian dubhs* with simple horn or plastic handles for day wear; the more elegant evening wear models have carved ebony handles, silver fittings and jeweled pommels.
11. *Shoes* – While any shoe will do with day wear—and you can wear regular dress shoes for evening wear—there are kilt shoe styles to consider. The most common is the ghillie brogue. This is a tongueless leather shoe with long laces to be tied around the ankle. Ghillie brogues go well with day wear or evening wear. You will find the laces tied in many ways, but the most common is to first twist them about three times, cross at the back of the ankle, and then tie in front or just off-center on the outside front of the lower shin. There is also the Mary Jane, a black leather shoe with anklet strap, which can go with evening wear or full dress. Full dress shoes often have large silver buckles on top, more for ornamentation than for function.

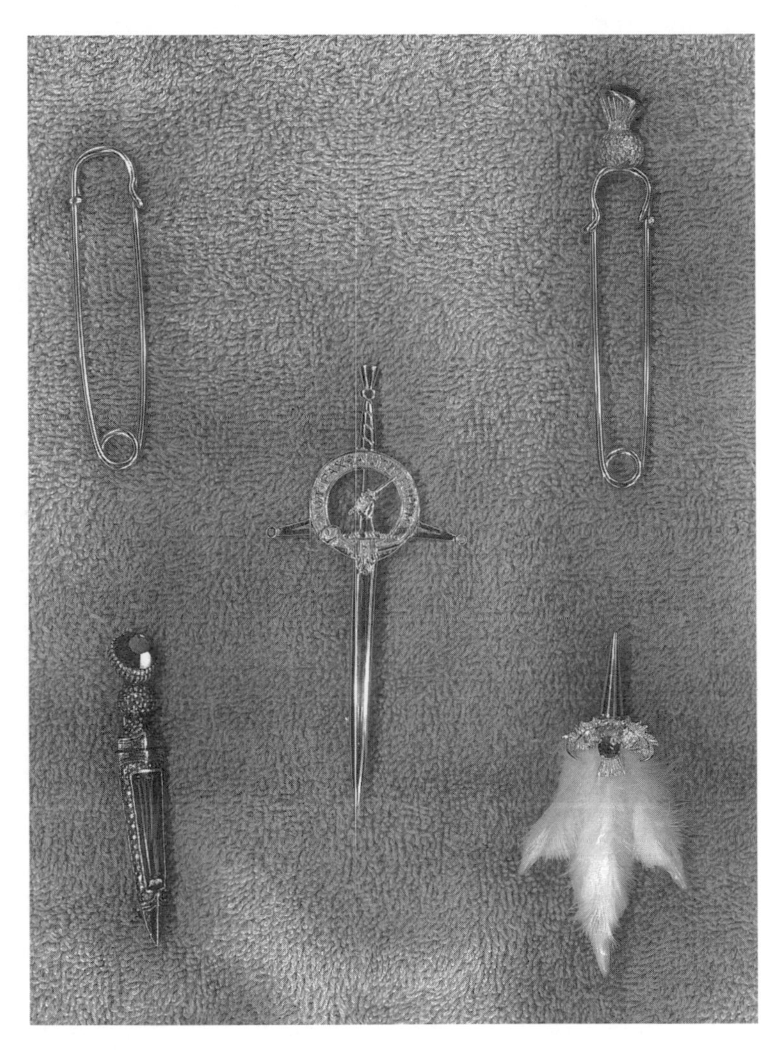

A sampling of kilt pins, from simple to highly ornate.

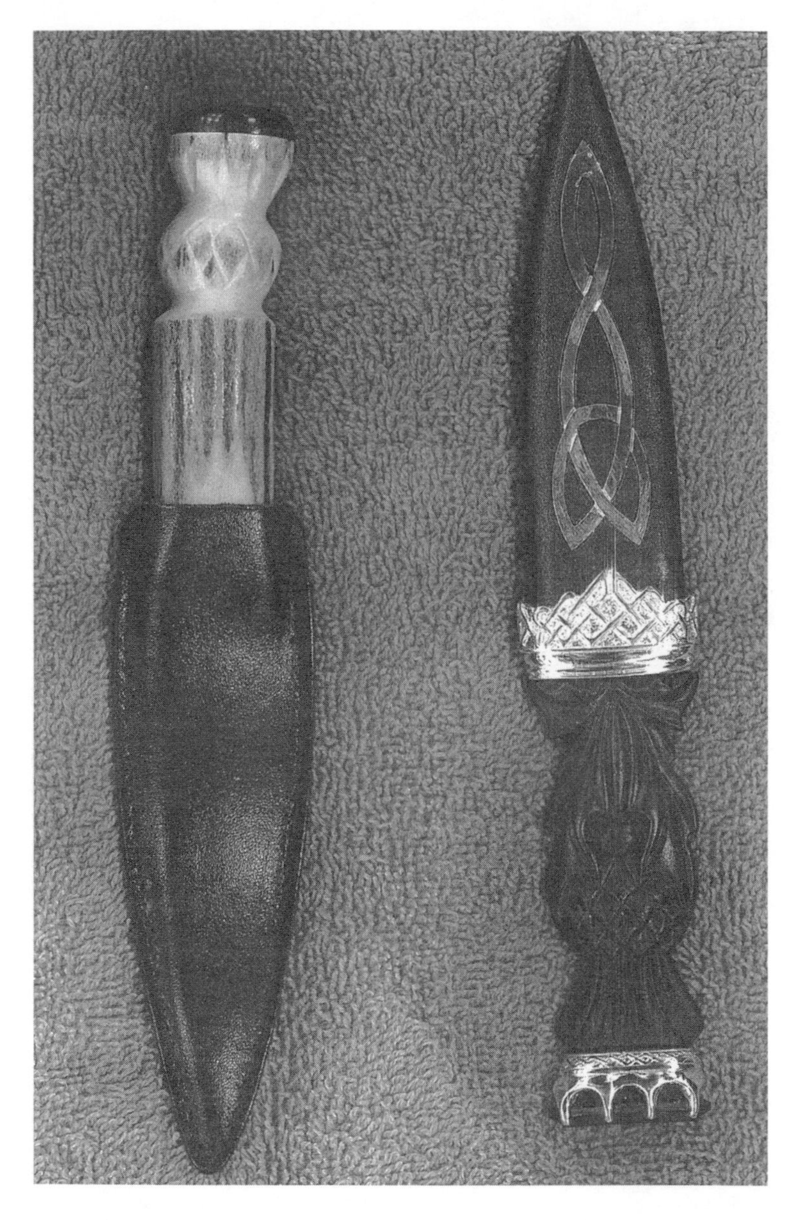

Two examples of sgian dubh, *the small knife worn in the hose top. The left is worn for day wear. The right with black handle and jeweled pommel is for evening wear or full dress.*

Now that you have a basic idea of Highland attire, the next step is to find where to buy or rent your outfits. Scottish import shops are not as numerous as tuxedo shops or bridal boutiques, but they often do mail-order business. One invaluable source for finding such shops is *The Highlander* magazine. Along with the classified ads listed in the bi-monthly issues, the magazine publishes a directory every April listing numerous outfitters and other vendors of Scottish attire. I have listed a few of these shops in the "References and Resources" section in the back of this book. Renting is often the best option if you do not see yourself wearing a kilt again. When choosing what type of attire for the groom's attendants, keep things coordinated. Do not have one wearing a black Argyll jacket with gauntlet cuffs, another with a Prince Charlie with military cuffs, and a third in a Montrose doublet. The groom, of course, can dress more formally than his groomsmen, so don't worry there. If you are a guest renting an ensemble, you don't necessarily have to rent formal evening wear. A good day wear jacket will do, just as a well-cut business suit is appropriate for attending a regular formal wedding. Also make sure that you order well ahead of time, especially if the wedding will be in a busy season like summer or Christmas; I would recommend placing your order six months in advance.

Rented Scottish attire will not come with shirts and ties, so you will have to purchase those. For evening wear, wing-tipped collars are more elegant than turndown collars, and black tie is definitely preferred. With a regulation doublet, you should go white tie, and you will need a lace jabot shirt to go with a high-necked doublet. If you are a guest wearing a day wear jacket, go with a regular white dress shirt and a tie in a solid color that will complement the colors of the kilt. Also, you should buy your woolen hose rather than rent them. Would you rent used socks from a tuxedo place? Of course not! Besides, you never know when you may need warm woolen stockings again.

As elegant as the kilt looks, there will likely be a fellow who insists: "NO WAY! I'm not wearing THAT!" Well, there are always alternatives. You can have vests, cummerbunds or bow ties made in tartan fabric; they are often found ready-made in some of the more commonly used tartans. More traditionally, there are the *trews*—dress pants made in tartan—which can be worn in place of a kilt with a Prince Charlie coat and vest, or as part of a tuxedo. Tartan neckties are appropriate for guests wearing business suits or sports jackets. Of course, guests and relatives are not required to wear tartan, but offering options may encourage them to do so and thus enhance the entire atmosphere of the wedding.

Wedding Luck

The Highlanders had many practices for bringing good fortune and warding off evil. Whether to believe them or not is up to you. Nonetheless, this chapter explores some of these unique traditions for assuring good luck, fertility and a happy marriage.

Prior to the marriage, friends of the bride and groom would playfully wash their feet and legs from knees to toes. A wedding ring was thrown into the wash basin, and whoever found it was said to be the next to marry.

Similar traditions revolved around the wedding cake. Trinkets were often baked inside the cake, each with a different meaning. A variation of this continued in the southern United States, with the trinkets attached to ribbons and pulled out by the bridesmaids. Female guests would also take a wedding ring and crumble some cake through it for luck in finding their true love.

Celtic societies also have a strong belief in traveling "sunwise"—from right to left to assure good fortune. People would even pass wine and stir porridge in the direction of the sun. Young women would run sunwise around the churchyard scattering hempseed, hoping to find their true love; brides often walked sunwise about the church before entering for the wedding.

To assure no bar to fertility, the bride and groom should have no knots on their person during the wedding day. The knots could be tied right after the ceremony, however, and this is where the term "tying the knot" supposedly comes from. In the event that a bride may be cursed by a jilted suitor, the groom would put a sixpence in his left shoe and leave that shoe untied. Such a curse, in fact, was made by the ex-suitor tying knots onto some colored threads.

I have already mentioned that green is considered an unlucky color. If your tartan has green in it, I wouldn't worry too much; my guess is that this applies to dressing in green from head to toe. Blue, on the other hand, is considered the color for fidelity.

Iron was thought to bring good luck. Marrying over an iron anvil is considered lucky, as well as presenting a horseshoe to the bride. Certain stones are also said to be charged with such power—a remnant from the days of the Druids.

Silver coins were also lucky. A custom common to bride and groom is to have a sixpence or other silver coin in the left shoe, putting on the right shoe first. Silver coins are also thrown to children on the way to the wedding. This comes from the "wedding ball" that was tossed by the bride before she set out for church. Eventually the ball was replaced by ball money, which was more than likely spent on something edible.

Mirrors had even more power; they were used in divining who one's future spouse would be, they were covered during a birth or death, and they were never looked into by the bride when she was fully dressed in her wedding gown.

Salt was thought to ward off evil, most likely derived from its purifying effect. Brides-to-be were taken around the town carrying a chamberpot full of salt, with passersby taking some for luck. Slipping salt into the groom's pocket without him seeing you was thought to bring him luck. And before the couple entered their new home, salt was scattered on the floor—especially around the bed.

After the wedding ceremony, the church bells were rung to scare away malevolent spirits. In lieu of bells, men would fire pistols into the air for the same effect. Church bells pealing survives throughout the British Isles as a way to send off the couple as they leave the church.

Finally, it is considered extremely bad luck for the bride to trip while entering her new home. This is much harder to avoid than you might think, given that the threshold to a door is often raised higher than the floor. The solution was for her new husband to carry her over the threshold, and that custom has persisted to date among Scots and non-Scots alike.

Paying the Piper (And Other Professionals)

Along with the guests and attendants at your wedding will be a host of professionals who will be working to make the whole event a memorable one. It is not enough to arrange for beautiful flowers, great music, delicious food and perfect pictures. You want to be confident and comfortable with the people *behind* those details.

General Guidelines

First of all, where do you find these people? Referrals from family and friends are your first source. Professional associations can also give you lists of contacts, and service providers in one field are more than happy to recommend someone in another with whom they have worked in the past. Interview your potential candidates and ask for written references. Ask to see, hear or taste samples of their work, and request a copy of their standard contract or letter of agreement. If a potential vendor cannot provide references, will not offer samples of his or her work, and refuses to put things in writing, *look somewhere else!* When you have chosen with whom you want to work, let them know as soon as possible. You should have all of these professionals retained about four to six months before the wedding date.

Most professional vendors ask for a deposit up front; pay with a credit card if they take them, both for record-keeping and security (it is easier to get a refund if need be). Keep in touch with your vendors and make sure that they understand *exactly* what you are looking for. Confirm everything about two weeks before the wedding, and provide them all with clear directions to the ceremony and reception. And, for any vendors who work during the reception, talk to the caterer to assure that they will be fed as well.

Another matter is gratuities. Some contracts, especially for catering, will include this in the total bill. If not, the best man should dispense the tips to the banquet manager, bartender, limousine driver, delivery people, et cetera. The only exceptions are parking valets and coatroom attendants; this is often prearranged with the facility management.

Musicians

In choosing a bagpiper, make sure that you choose a quality musician with experience performing at weddings. Ask if the piper is a member of the United States Pipe Band Association (USPBA) or a regional body. If so, what is his or her grade? Grade IV is beginners, and Grade I is the highest; professionals are usually Grade I or II, although there are excellent amateurs as well. Ask if you can listen to an audition tape, or better yet, hear them perform. Discuss what tunes they know and which they feel would be appropriate to play. Keep in mind that pipers have different styles and use a variety of chanters and drones to produce different voices. Ask about their attire as well. If your overall wedding attire is informal or Jacobean, a white shirt will do. For formal settings, he or she should wear either evening wear or full dress, or a piper's tunic with plumed bonnet, horsehair sporran and other accoutrements. The piper will also have questions about his or her role in the program. Will the piper play in the church or outside? Processional, recessional, or both? Interlude music? Music for the reception? Let the piper know exactly what you have in mind for the wedding. My personal preference is for the piper to lead the processional and recessional at the ceremony, then to lead the couple as they enter the reception. Realistically, however, there may be restrictions in acoustic quality or facility regulations. The best acoustics for the great bagpipes (other than out-of-doors) is a large, airy sanctuary with a high ceiling. If your church is a cozy little chapel with a low ceiling, your guests will better appreciate small pipes, a scaled-down version with a lower volume, or the great pipes played outside the church.

For other parts of the ceremony, you and your spouse-to-be should discuss what kind of music you want—instrumental or vocal, solo or ensemble, classical, popular, or folk. Come up with two or three alternatives, then begin researching and interviewing. Two specific pieces of advice. First, if you decide on the church organ, stick to an instrumentalist approved by the church; pipe organs are very delicate instruments, and not everyone can play them. Second, if a friend or family member offers to sing or play—unless they are very good and offer the sound that you want—politely turn them down. One final note: if you want your piper and other musicians to play at the rehearsal (which is a very good idea), inquire whether they charge extra.

Music for the reception can be a jazz band, a deejay, or a Scottish *ceilidh* band with fiddle, accordion and drum. In some cases, you may be able to have one or two reception band members play at the ceremony and save some money, but more likely you will be hiring separate acts. Decide what kind of sound you want, and whether to go with live or recorded music. Then start looking for and interviewing band leaders or deejays, again requesting auditions or video demos whenever possible. Along with their music, remember to keep their dress and deportment in mind. Find out if they have any particular needs for electrical wiring, staging, and so on. Go over the play list—and the *do-not-play* list—with prospective musicians before contracting them.

Caterers and Bakers

Some reception sites will have their own catering staff and require you to work with them. Others will provide a list of preferred caterers to work with. If you have to look for one yourself, start with references from friends and family. (I have frequently dropped the name of a friend from church who caters weddings and other events.) Another alternative, and the most ingenious I have heard of, was used by a friend of mine. He and his wife contacted a culinary arts school to cater their wedding; they got terrific food at a fraction of the cost, and the students obtained some hands-on experience.

Before you interview caterers, decide what kind of reception you want: simple cake and punch, afternoon or high tea, a buffet, or a banquet. The more elaborate the setup, the more wait staff required, and the higher the expense. Ask caterers for sample menus, and whether they can prepare any personal favorites or traditional Scottish dishes if you provide the recipes. Also inquire whether a caterer can bake your wedding cake, or recommend a baker.

Many wedding receptions, especially in the southern United States, have both the traditional wedding cake and a large groom's cake with some sort of theme decoration. When checking a baker, ask about whether they use fresh cakes or frozen, and what flavors and designs they offer. Most bakers will deliver the cake for an extra charge, and may even cut and serve the cakes for you; if they do not do the serving, your caterer most likely will. For a Scottish or tartan theme, ask about what kind of special decoration they can do. For example, the House of Scotland in Ontario, Canada (see under "References and Resources") offers tartan wedding cake toppers with kilted grooms! This is the only shop I know of to sell this creative cake decoration. As an alternative, you will find that most local, talented cake decorators can do just about anything with icing and marzipan. Many wedding cakes are decorated with flowers, either real or sculpted confiture, so you may want the baker and florist to coordinate their efforts.

Once you have selected the caterer and baker, remember to give them a precise head count of the number of guests, including musicians, photographers and others. This is important, as they typically charge per person, so *don't guess!* You should have these numbers about two to four weeks before the wedding. Caterers usually make about 10 to 25 percent more food than requested, so see whether they will agree to some leeway in the event that you have fewer guests show up.

Florist or Decorator

Florists and decorators now go by many terms, including floral designer and event planner. Before you call, decide on how much you are willing to spend for flowers and decorations. Will you decorate the ceremony site, the reception site, or both? Simple or elaborate? If you do both, can you transport some of the ceremony decorations to the reception?

Take extra care in checking the references and qualifications of any florist or decorator. You will be relying on their expertise and guidance much more than any other professional, so make sure that you can trust him or her completely.

The florist will likely want to look over the site or sites to be decorated. Be prepared to give him or her other detailed information about the tartan used in your wedding, the fabric and design of your wedding gown and the bridesmaids' dresses, and so forth. Ask the florist or decorator about delivery, setup, and labeling bouquets and boutonnieres for attendants.

Photographer

Wedding photography is as much an art as music or floral decoration. One increasingly popular trend is a "photojournalist" style that focuses on emotion-filled candid shots, often in black and white. Candid shots can look great, whether color or black-and-white, but *color* photos capture the real beauty of tartan better than black and white. Also, the precision and special film required for good black-and-white photos make them actually more expensive than color. When interviewing photographers, look at samples of both their formal posed shots (often called "portraiture") and candid pictures. Read the contract carefully before signing, and make sure as well that you are dealing with the person who will actually take the pictures. That photographer should also do a site inspection to get an idea of the lighting conditions.

Limousine

Whether transporting the wedding party between the ceremony and the reception, or providing an intimate getaway for the bride and groom, a limousine adds to the elegance of the occasion. Part of this elegance is the attire of the driver, who should be appropriately dressed in a dark uniform. But nothing can spoil the moment more than your chariot being late! So, when contracting your car and driver, make sure that you pin down such particulars as pick-up time, destination, and any extra services such as drinks (if allowed). Many vendors recommend that you contract for a little longer than the standard rental period, just to be on the safe side.

The most appealing alternative to a limousine or antique motorcar is the horse and carriage. Very romantic—and very expensive. The main reason for the expense is that the companies that rent them are required to carry liability insurance. Along with the questions you would ask a limousine company, ask the carriage company about the cost and terms of this insurance.

A Final Note

The rapport and relationship you have with your wedding professionals is as important as the services they provide. That it or not, you need a little of both! Yes, you need the flexible and creative side to find the proper balance, but you also need the more obstinate purists to make sure that things are still done right.

A simple approach is to have the wedding ceremony in one cultural theme, and the reception in another. This sounds simple, but there are some problems to consider. First of all, it could be a shock to your guests. Imagine walking on a road through the Scottish heath, turning a corner, and winding up in Mexico City or Tokyo (or, the other way around). Secondly, one family may be offended at the suggestion of having their culture relegated to just the reception. Third, and in my view most important, this divided celebration goes against the very idea of marriage as *uniting* two people and two lives into a new family, drawing on the experience and strength of both.

My suggestion is to focus on the ceremony and let the reception be thoroughly North American. I have already stated the view that bagpipes and the wearing of tartan (preferably the kilt) are the minimum for a tartan wedding. The reason is obvious: these are the most easily recognized symbols of Scottish heritage. Now, following the same line of reasoning, find two easily identifiable symbols of the non-Scottish family heritage which you could incorporate into your wedding. It could be anything from clothing or music to a particular ritual or the meaning ascribed to a certain color.

Interfaith weddings have additional concerns. Will you marry in a house of worship or in a more "neutral" setting? Will you choose one officiant, or two co-officiants? Will your respective religious communities even approve of marrying outside your faith? In some cases, couples have chosen to have two ceremonies, one according to each tradition. Others have said "To heck with it!" and have chosen a civil ceremony or progressive non-creedal denomination like the Ethical Culture movement or the Unitarian-Universalist Association.

relationship runs both ways. Treat them with the respect and professionalism they deserve, and they will respond with their best. Treat them like month-old haggis and . . . well, you get the idea.

And Now, For Something Completely Different

Many wedding traditions are rooted in assumptions of religion, ethnicity and gender. In the past, it was assumed that you married "your own kind," that marriage was forever, that the bride had all female attendants and the groom all male, and that a bride married a groom and vice versa. Now we have found that our ancestors' assumptions are not so true, and still we wish to honor the heritage they provide us through tradition. So, this chapter is devoted to finding a way around all those assumptions.

Mixed Heritage Weddings

You are getting married, and you and your family would like to have a full-fledged tartan wedding. Then the parents of your intended say: "What about *our* culture? Why all this 'Scottish this' and 'Scottish that'? Nothing wrong with Scotland, mind you, but we're proud of our background, too, you know!"

Good point. There is no reason why you can't celebrate two or more cultural or religious backgrounds. Many times customs and traditions overlap, which can make things easier. Other times, when the traditions in question are quite different, incorporating a little of each can be just enough to make the wedding your own. The real trick, as I see it, would be the personalities of your families—some will be stubborn and narrow-minded, others will be flexible and creative. And, believe relationship runs both ways. Treat them with the respect and professionalism they deserve, and they will respond with their best. Treat them like month-old haggis and . . . well, you get the idea.

And Now, For Something Completely Different

Many wedding traditions are rooted in assumptions of religion, ethnicity and gender. In the past, it was assumed that you married "your own kind," that marriage was forever, that the bride had all female attendants and the groom all male, and that a bride married a groom and vice versa. Now we have found that our ancestors' assumptions are not so true, and still we wish to honor the heritage they provide us through tradition. So, this chapter is devoted to finding a way around all those assumptions.

Mixed Heritage Weddings

You are getting married, and you and your family would like to have a full-fledged tartan wedding. Then the parents of your intended say: "What about *our* culture? Why all this 'Scottish this' and 'Scottish that'? Nothing wrong with Scotland, mind you, but we're proud of our background, too, you know!"

Good point. There is no reason why you can't celebrate two or more cultural or religious backgrounds. Many times customs and traditions overlap, which can make things easier. Other times, when the traditions in question are quite different, incorporating a little of each can be just enough to make the wedding your own. The real trick, as I see it, would be the personalities of your families—some will be stubborn and narrow-minded, others will be flexible and creative. And, believe it or not, you need a little of both! Yes, you need the flexible and creative side to find the proper balance, but you also need the more obstinate purists to make sure that things are still done right.

A simple approach is to have the wedding ceremony in one cultural theme, and the reception in another. This sounds simple, but there are some problems to consider. First of all, it could be a shock to your guests. Imagine walking on a road through the Scottish heath, turning a corner, and winding up in Mexico City or Tokyo (or, the other way around). Secondly, one family may be offended at the suggestion of having their culture relegated to just the reception. Third, and in my view most important, this divided celebration goes against the very idea of marriage as *uniting* two people and two lives into a new family, drawing on the experience and strength of both.

My suggestion is to focus on the ceremony and let the reception be thoroughly North American. I have already stated the view that bagpipes and the wearing of tartan (preferably the kilt) are the minimum for a tartan wedding. The reason is obvious: these are the most easily recognized symbols of Scottish heritage. Now, following the same line of reasoning, find two easily identifiable symbols of the non-Scottish family heritage which you could incorporate into your wedding. It could be anything from clothing or music to a particular ritual or the meaning ascribed to a certain color.

Interfaith weddings have additional concerns. Will you marry in a house of worship or in a more "neutral" setting? Will you choose one officiant, or two co-officiants? Will your respective religious communities even approve of marrying outside your faith? In some cases, couples have chosen to have two ceremonies, one according to each tradition. Others have said "To heck with it!" and have chosen a civil ceremony or progressive non-creedal denomination like the Ethical Culture movement or the Unitarian-Universalist Association.